With love
Diana Tennys—

CW01099716

LOVING FOR LOVERS

LOVING FOR LOVERS

Diana Tennyson

Book Guild Publishing
Sussex, England

First published in Great Britain in 2010 by
The Book Guild Ltd
Pavilion View
19 New Road
Brighton, BN1 1UF

Typesetting in Bembo by
Keyboard Services, Luton, Bedfordshire

Printed in Great Britain by
CPI Antony Rowe

A catalogue record for this book is available from
The British Library

ISBN 978 1 84624 391 2

In Memoriam
Heather Margaret Quine
1952–2000

CONTENTS

DREAM

Rose Garden, Polesden Lacey

I dream I watch whilst you're asleep,
Watch over you for countless hours
Your mind traversing oceans deep,
Or garden paths festooned with flowers.

I dream I kiss your gentle eyes,
And see you stir recalling me
Your mind traversing sunlit skies,
Remembers, and is all to me.

EXMOOR ESTUARY

I am looking for the birds
In the gap where the tide comes in,
Yesterday they were here,
Diving and dipping in the waves,
But today it is deserted.

A small child plays on the sand
In the gap where the tide comes in,
Digging for shells and dreams,
Liquid sand sucking toes,
Drawing her down.

Waves ripple and run with the wind
In the gap where the tide comes in,
Creeping across the sand,
Where land becomes fluid,
Flowing with the sea.

Waves breaking evenly and rain falling steadily
In the gap where the tide comes in,
Fast flowing now, submerging me,
Releasing the pain
That's destroying me.

...BUT SOMETIMES

Here I am again
crushing your shells
treading on water -

       Holding your hands
       heeding your words
       loving you always
       trying not to look back
       'else I stumble and crumble
       and fail everyone.

              But sometimes I need
              someone to hold me
              someone to love me
              and someone to love.

I am here today
as I always am
ready and waiting –

       Fulfilling my role
       not shirking the pain
       or the stress
       that you're under
       returning your calls
       your hugs and your kisses.

3

But sometimes I need
someone to talk to
someone to laugh with
and dance until dawn.

I'm always here
counting the raindrops
drying your tears -

Trying to listen
absorbing your pain
praising successes
building you up
not knocking you down
with a smile not a frown.

But sometimes I need
some warmth and affection
or my dreams will desert me
and I'll dry up and wither.

It's not love divided
it's the strength I rely on
and you know the answer –

We all need a future
and the present is now
I cannot control you
own or direct you
and we all need some space
to make our decisions.

But sometimes I need
a hard wall to hit on
someone to sustain me
and take all my pain.

4

BAILERO (from 'Songs of the Auvergne')

I sit alone each day beneath the sun
Rays flicker, caressing golden brown,
Water falls sparkling into an edifying tomb,
The grasses high in meadows where I walk
I snatch a distant murmur –
Was that your voice, or was I only dreaming?

> He that loves shall always love
> And he that desires will have no part,
> The waters and the grasses will pull me under
> Whilst the fingers of the sun will warm my heart
> The shadows fall 'neath aged trees
> Was that our song, an echo on the breeze?

So many seem to need me now,
Is it warmth, presence, desire to fill?
Loved and yet unloved, I tumble with the wind,
A gentle kiss that lingered on your mouth
The taste, a memory you hold within –
Your touch, a gentle brush against my skin.

> And now I travel through the night,
> The solitary moon, the only dancer on the floor,
> She and I see eye to eye,
> But with you, there's something more:
> Flying homewards, I need you near,
> But that touch, caress is never here.

BEAUTY OF THE NIGHT

In the beauty of the night
There seems no movement
Save the light
That plays on window,
Stair and screen
With light, and dark, and in between.

All shadows merging into one
Forming shapes that dawn
Disperses when day
Returns and sunlight burns
The ashes that so oft are strewn
On pathways and amongst the ferns.

The day is new, the dawn has come
And life goes on beneath the sun.
But night, my friend, has faded fast,
Its velvet softness cannot last,
Or hide what I must cherish here
My love for one I hold most dear.

CANDLES OF HOPE

At Petworth Park

Time within an hourglass slipping away
Like golden sand between my golden fingers,
And here and there sunlight and reflections
Caught and held in misty mirrors
To cast a spell on dingy paintings,
Desperate ghosts looming wide-eyed,
Imprisoned in frames in darkened hallways
An era long since gone, a parting yesteryear,
Remote, dormant and entombed in dust.

But out beyond the chapel walls
A tree of blossom and of hope,
White, austere, bedecked in blooms
A candelabra weighed down with light
And each pale globe yet barely open
About to burst and shine
As in the phases of the moon;
Pale ornaments opaque as petals pressed
Palm to palm in paradise and perfect prayer.

And now whilst sitting in sunlight
Crossed-legged on grassy slopes,
My thoughts are of you, my dearest,
A light shining deep within my soul
And comforting my darkest nights;
You alone are my candle of hope,

7

My candle of infinite joy,
For I will never waiver or be fickle
As in the phases of the moon.

Let me destroy those desperate ghosts,
And replace them with my perfect love
On which you may rely, my dearest,
To be the light shining within your soul
Dispelling your fears and all thoughts of sadness;
I alone am your candle of hope,
And your candle of infinite joy,
To hold you so closely, love you so deeply
And send you to paradise.

'Lovers are the richest on the Earth,
Their admirers are the Mighty
Never to approach, but like Jove
In a shower of Gold –'

CLOSE OF DAY

The day has turned from golden
Into blood-red hues
And that small thread
That binds us is stretched –
Time is immense
And distance so vast
The sun is now setting
And shadows are cast.

The twilight has turned from blood red
Into violet darkness
And that small thread
That binds us could break –
Time is infinite
And each hour so long
These petals can crush me
And then I'll be gone.

COME

Come to me at this late hour
Take my heart and let me
Make yours mine again –
      Let spring's green mantle
      Take away your sorrow
And let the summer on my lips
Warm your blood and send it
Coursing through your veins.
      Let me kiss your eyes
      Until they gape so wide awake
They close with sheer exhaustion
Whilst I take you in my arms
Bestow on you such wondrous kisses –
      And with my subtle charms
      I'll break you gently with such pain
You'll wake and beg for love and pain,
And beg for pain and love again
And love and pain again –

THE GIFT

He gives to you his heart,
His heart is yours –
He gives you all his love,
His love is yours –

      And through all this turmoil
      He tries so hard to give you
      All his strength,
      All his support –
      And he gives today
      These hours together
      Because they are precious
      And you never know
      When your time
      Might be snatched away.

He gives you his dreams,
His dreams are yours –
He gives you all his life,
His life is yours.

      And through all this turmoil
      He wants so much to share
      All his dreams,
      All his visions –
      And he gives you today
      These hours together

This clear blue sky
And this gift of life and love,
The calm within his soul
That cannot be snatched away.

ADUMBRATION

I'm slipping through your fingers
But please don't let me fall.
I'm reaching to capture your soul
But your armour prevents
Penetration.

Lips and eyes may speak of love
But you have no wish to possess,
So I'm drifting out to sea because
I could never give you less
Than Me.

Catch me as I drift on by,
My heart's both sincere and true,
Although I'm held behind glass
And unable to pass, I only have eyes
For You.

RETREAT

Sunset call on Bugle

You're only a dream away,
Aren't you?
Only a whisper
From my ear
And only one heartbeat
From mine.

But you're a thunderclap
Within my soul,
You're the poison
I've consumed,
And you're the passion
I give.

You're only a dream away,
Aren't you?
You're still there
When I open my eyes?
And I'll be in your arms
When I awake?

But you're the lightning
Striking my heart,
I hold nothing back
When you ask me,
And there's nothing I can't give
When you love me.

14

THERE ARE DREAMS...

There are dreams and other dreams,
And times when thoughts run wild –
Forgive me for loving you too much
For I am oft' beguiled.

And there are thoughts and other thoughts,
And times when time stands still –
Forgive me for loving you too much
And never wish me ill.

And there are moments I recall
How close you are to me –
Is this a vision, thought or dream
You'll make reality?

EACH NIGHT

Each night you leave me
Lying sleeping –
The hours that pass
Won't find me weeping,
The morning sun
Won't find me grieving,
You couldn't stay,
So you're not leaving...

Each night you leave me
Lying dreaming –
The days that pass
Have little meaning
The morning sun
Still finds me sighing,
You couldn't come,
So I'm not crying...

FINALE

That part of you was part of me
As oceans part, no dream I see,
My world is turning into dust,
I lived, I loved and now I must
Depart and never backward glance
For I shall wander in a trance –
I have no life, no love to give,
It seems unjust, but I can't live
Or bear this pain, another knife,
And so in truth, I have no life.

In years to come, you will recall
That once I gave my life, my all,
But you betrayed and broke my heart,
My precious gift is torn apart.
I have no life, I'm full of grief,
Death beckons me, it's my relief –
I really can't take further pain,
I have no wish to love again.
I've gone, I've disappeared, I've vanished,
Now you've decreed that I am banished.

FRIDAY

On Friday we lay upon the floor
And loved each other yet once more,
Take this love to make it,
Why take this love to break it?

Tomorrow looms so dark and grey,
But very soon there'll be a day
When we are close, at one together,
So take this love to make it,
Why take this love to break it?

It's near, it's nearer than you think,
You're almost standing on the brink
And here you gaze with solemn looks,
At one who wrote and loved your books,
So take this love to make it,
Why take this love to break it?

HOW DO I LOVE YOU?

How do I love you?
And why do I care?
Questions with answers
Left floating in air.

The past is forgotten
The future is ours,
My feelings are kisses,
The raindrops in showers.

And life lies before us
So boundless and green,
Its vastness astounds me,
Its limits unseen.

When you ask me that question,
Or how do I feel,
I don't have the answer
Except that it's real.

Can I bring you joy?
Can I clasp your soul?
If you trust and let go
Then this can be whole.

STARLIGHT BY CANDLELIGHT

When days are short and darkness shrouds my world,
When sunlight eludes me and there's not a glimmer of hope,
When I wake early and walk about the house;
Watch starlight by candlelight to soften the blows.

When I must remain steadfast, sure and true,
When everyone about me flies to the wall,
When I must be the calm within the storm;
Watch starlight by candlelight to soften the blows.

When knives turn again and there's no one to cling to,
When the armies of hell line up before me,
When tears fill my eyes and burn my cheeks;
Watch starlight by candlelight to soften the blows.

When you tell me not to fear and keep calm,
When you hold me close to keep me from harm,
When I recall the world's a small orb in God's arms;
Watch starlight by candlelight to soften the blows.

HOW DO YOU WANT ME TO LOVE YOU?

How do you want me to love you,
How do I fit into your dreams?
How do you need me to want you,
Do I concur with your schemes?
How do you want me to feel about this,
Are you going to break me apart?
Or do we have each other forever,
And will you vouchsafe for my heart?

How do you want me to love you,
Am I here for a day or a year?
How do you need me to want you?
Please tell me there's nothing to fear.
How do you want me to feel about this?
Yet when I look into your eyes
I know we have each other forever
And I know that you'll tell me no lies.

I AM SHE

I am she
who waits alone today,
I am she
who hoped she wouldn't be
alone today,
I am she
who waits and watches rain,
And I am she
who thought she wouldn't be
alone again.

        I am she
        who loves you more and more
        each day,
        And I am she
        who cares so much it hurts
        in every way,
        I am she
        with tears in turquoise eyes,
        And I am she
        who cannot contemplate,
        so sits alone and cries.

                I am she
                who feels abandoned
                in the storm,
                And I am she

whom you once said
you'd never want to harm,
I am she
who needs to be
held safe and close by you,
And today I'm she
who can only be
The lady dressed in blue.

KISS AWAKE

Softly slumber
Sleeping softly
Gentle baby
Kiss awake.

Slumber softly
Tender touches
Warmly wanting
You awake.

Tender touches
Wanting warmly
Caressing kissing
You awake.

Gentle kisses
Sleepy darling
Softly kissing
You awake.

Softly sleeping
Kissing softly
Unresisting
Kiss awake.

Softly by you
Sleeping softly
Waiting wanting
Kiss awake.

LIKE CHRISTMAS

I awoke early this morning,
And it felt like Christmas,
I glowed with warmth and love
And didn't feel lost and lonely
Any more.

When I awoke early this morning,
And it felt like Christmas,
The world was dark
But the stars were shining
For me.

When I awoke early this morning,
And it felt like Christmas,
I couldn't stop crying
But I don't know why I shed
So many tears.

I read your letter at six a.m.
And it felt like Christmas,
You have given me a special gift
A gift of love and life
With you.

When I re-read your letter,
And it felt like Christmas,
Safe and secure in your love
Soon to be close to you
Forever.

When I thought of you this morning,
And it felt like Christmas,
I couldn't think of the future
Without your love and my love for you
In return.

LOVING YOU

There is no cure for loving you
Adoring you or giving you,
Or being close and holding you,
So deeply bound, a part of you.

There are no tears for missing you
Adoring you or needing you,
Or being miles apart from you,
Yet deeply bound, a part of you.

There is no pain in leaving you
Adoring you or meeting you,
Or being held and loved by you,
So deeply bound, a part of you.

There is no cure for loving you
But tears there are for needing you,
And pain there is for wanting you
And love there is for loving you,
More deeply bound, a part of you.

LOVE DAY

I loved finding you waiting for me,
I loved being in your arms,
I loved making you coffee
And not having time to drink it.
I loved sitting in your lap
And being kissed by you,
I loved holding your head in my arms
And gently stroking your hair.

I loved finding you in my bed,
I loved you holding me close,
I love you whispering your desire
And I loved you so near.
I loved kissing you there
And giving you my love —
I loved you loving me
And holding me afterwards.

I loved making you lunch,
I loved bringing you wine,
I loved finding you sleeping
To wake you with kisses.
I loved sitting with you
And touching you there,
I loved turning you on
And finding you wanting me.

I loved watching you eat,
I loved giving you dessert,
I loved lying with my head
In your lap and you kissing me.
I loved finding you naked on my bed
And you slipping under the covers,
I loved lying with my head on your chest
And treasuring the moment.

I loved you kissing me again,
I loved you giving to me,
I loved holding you tightly afterwards
And feeling you quake inside me.
I loved you telling me
You love me more and more
And I loved saying, I love you –
And I love being with you.

I loved walking with you,
I loved you holding back a branch,
I loved you holding my hand
And talking to me.
I loved you telling me your fears
Because they are mine,
I loved you giving me your grief
Because that is mine also.

I hated saying goodbye,
I hated you driving away,
I hated you disappearing from view
And I hated driving away from you.

I hate being here today without you,
Waking and lying in this bed alone,
I hate writing you these words
Instead of speaking them to you.

I hate being alone and surrounded by people,
I hate knowing we're apart for so long,
I hate talking to my friends on the phone
And not being able to say, I have you.
I hate the grey of today
And wanting you in my arms,
I hate feeling empty
And wanting you beside me.

I love the memory of you forever,
I love you giving me some hope,
I love you making plans
And telling me your aspirations.
I love you touching my soul
And I want to wake with you beside me,
I love to dream of you
And never wake up.

I love you more than any words can say,
I love you in every way possible,
I love you with all my tears
And I never want to let you go.
I love you with all my hopes of tomorrow
And our future together,
I love you with all my heart −
As if you ever had to doubt it.

MAKE IT REAL

The days are growing longer
And the sun's back in the sky,
The long dark days of winter
Are quickly rushing by,
And with the hope of springtime
Come dreams that you can feel
And you only have to love
To make it real.

Take the joy I bring you,
Ask me for nothing more,
I'm the hope in your bright future
And what you're striving for,
I'm a ray of sun and showers
With me you know you feel
And you only have to love
To make it real.

MORE OR LESS

More than this I need you,
More than this I care,
More than love to give you
And more than love to share.

More than arms to hold you,
More than being near,
More than us together
Because I hold you dear.

Less I cannot give you,
Less is far apart,
Less is never with you
And less divides my heart.

Less is waking lonely,
Less is never there,
Less always says, if only
You were here to share.

MORNING RAIN

A day ago you left me,
The hours pass slowly by –
Raindrops gather overhead
With thunderclaps and I
    Feel raindrops falling
    through my heart
    to soothe each heavy sigh.

      You say that you should be here,
      You never should have gone –
      But you are safe inside my heart
      Throughout each summer storm.
          Rain can never wash away
          and storms cannot undo,
          but time serves only to recall
          the hours spent missing you.

            And now I wonder
            Where you are –
            I'm walking on my own
            Through woods and fields and flowers,
               past churches built of stone,
               past graves of those who went away
               and did not want to go,
               or miss the rains of summer,
               and walks through woods in snow.

SNOWFLAKE

Snowflake came last night,
She lived
And loved
And died.
She was heaven sent
And came to give us life
But now she is
The tears
In our eyes.

BENEATH THE STARS

I thought I woke with you last night,
And we held hands,
And walked a while beneath the stars,
The night was cloudless
Bright and clear.

And you and I paused once to kiss
And you held my face,
And we walked a while beneath the stars,
You holding my eyes in yours
And my heart in your hands.

SORROW

Rain is falling from the skies,
Tears are falling from my eyes,
So much torment racks my heart
Tearing me, my world apart.

The Christmas lights that gleam and glow,
Are but my blood upon the snow,
I give to you the purest love,
Peace of mind, the whitest dove.

Distant music in the rain,
Rhythm patters on the pane,
So much grief within my heart
Tearing me, my world apart.

I hardly know which way to turn,
A heart on fire with love to burn,
But everything you give to me
Perhaps one day will set you free.

SOLACE

The veil of summer lifts and rests on open seas
And mists of autumn envelop valleys and the changing trees –
But you are safe, and sound at every dawn
Oblivious to the world and clamour of the storm.

Let me take you to my hidden valley by the sea
Where spring comes early and winter barely sighs –
And you can rest in sunlight beneath tender leaves
And watch the seabirds wheel in pale blue skies.

Sleep soft within your lush green bower
Let anger dissipate and loosen from your mind –
And the scent of earth and rain and bracken overcome you
Whilst the ropes about your arms loosen and unbind.

Come with me and rest on smooth, grey rocks to watch the
    changing sea,
The rugged cliffs and anxious trees blown against the hill –
Watch waves and foam, and light and dark
Until the sun slips slowly out of sight and all is still.

Sleep safe and deeply in my hidden valley,
Cast aside your worries and your fears –
Only know that you are safe, secure and well
And your eyes no longer full of tears.

THE VOID

I can see what this place was like,
How you loved being here,
And how you were loved;
And when that love deserted you
You lost your soul.

I can see that you loved this place,
You built the waterfall,
And watched fish swim in the sunlight;
The hours full of happiness
And too full to count.

I can see that you carved these creatures,
And the clocks looked down,
Ticking slowly through time;
Till time caught up with you
And there was no more time.

TO MY LOVE

Each morning when the sun will rise
I raise my hand to shade my eyes
And looking out across the lawn
I watch the early morning dawn.
I can't believe the words you say
And yet repeat them day by day,
Tell me that after this short time,
Is it true your heart is mine?

The rising sun in satin skies
Is mirrored in your gentle eyes
And all the world is filled with song
The dawn will chorus all day long.
If I could only put to words
The singing of a thousand birds,
Those words would be but very few,
How much in love I am with you.

WHEN THE SUN SHINES AGAIN

How will it be when the sun shines again,
Will the pain become any less?
Will the 'you' that I miss
Remain here to kiss
Away tears in my eyes
And the rain in the skies ... And

How will you feel when the sun shines again,
When the mists in the valleys disperse?
Will our love be as strong
As the summer day's long
And the joy in your eyes
Will be no surprise. ... But

Will you be here when the rain falls again,
Will you stay and never depart?
Because the 'me' that you need
Would suffer and bleed
If you want me this way
And then threw me away ... If

I'm here with the smiles, and the tears, and the rain,
And this love that's so precious is ours –
Will you stay in my heart
Never break it apart –
Send me love every day
With your flowers ...

WORDS

The sunrise is golden
    breaking at dawn,
Brings light to my heart
    but leaves me forlorn,
When your words are so harsh
    and your voice full of pain
You crush this small shell
    again and again.

My gifts may be few
    but their value is high,
I can wipe away pain
    and the clouds from your sky,
I bring gold at dawn
    and light to your heart
But my courage will fail
    if you tear me apart.

I'm high in your tower
    but you're not there today –
Winds of change draw me up
    and could blow me away.

YOU HAVEN'T LONG

You said yourself you haven't long
What little time will soon be gone
What little love you haven't won
The Moody Blues still sing your song.

All the things you said you'd do,
All the plans you made anew
The love you said you had would grow
So sad it wasn't there, we know.

The sorrow in her heart remains
The hopes she cherished stay the same
The happy times that she had known
Thrown to the sea to sink like stone.

EREBUS

Dull grey day, so dark with skies filled with snow,
Ground sodden and soaked like sponge,
And we're complaining like the 'camel men',
Cursing the weather and the company.

Trees weeping silently into the stream,
Gorged with torrents from the hills,
And we're dicing at the doorway
With six pieces of silver.

The heron floating like a galleon
Through islands of grey cloud
Espies an old grey horse
Galloping away in a meadow.

A handful of travellers following a star,
A group of lonely shepherds drawn to a stable,
The 'camel men' wanting their 'liquor and women'
Are as blind as we are.

Going around in circles like the old grey horse,
Galloping nowhere, out of time and out of tune,
Dark days rushing in with rain and tears ...
The beginning was the end and remains so ...

(Inspired by 'Journey of the Magi' by T.S. Eliot)